You Never Said. We Didn't Ask:

A Legacy from World War I

poems by

Estella Lauter

Finishing Line Press
Georgetown, Kentucky

You Never Said.
We Didn't Ask:

A Legacy from
World War I

Dedicated to Charles F. Lauter, Jr. (Chuck)
and Nancy Goodman (1956-2016)
who kept the stories alive

Copyright © 2018 by Estella Lauter
ISBN 978-1-63534-502-5 First Edition
All rights reserved under International and Pan-American Copyright Conventions. No part of this book may be reproduced in any manner whatsoever without written permission from the publisher, except in the case of brief quotations embodied in critical articles and reviews.

ACKNOWLEDGMENTS

"A Legacy of WWI" received an honorable mention in the HaL Prize contest sponsored by *The Peninsula Pulse* in August 2014. The contest was judged by Heid E. Erdrich.

Publisher: Leah Maines
Editor: Christen Kincaid
Cover Art: Ann Heyse
Author Photo: Josephine Lauter Passananti
Cover Design: Elizabeth Maines McCleavy

Printed in the USA on acid-free paper.
Order online: www.finishinglinepress.com
    also available on amazon.com

Author inquiries and mail orders:
Finishing Line Press
P. O. Box 1626
Georgetown, Kentucky 40324
U. S. A.

Table of Contents

Legacy 1

The Thin Red Book 2

German American..4

Camp Upton, 1917 5

The USS Leviathan 6

Trials Galore—April—July, 1918.....................................7

Forty Men or Eight Horses..8

The Baccarat Decanter 9

Proving Your Worth..10

After the Vesle 11

The Eight-Day March, September 1918 12

Found Poetry 13

One of the few stories 14

After the Armistice..15

Unintended Consequences 16

Homecoming 17

The Photo Enigma 18

The Spoils of War..19

Why Didn't You Speak? 20

The Amnesia of War...21

Aftermath: Greene, N.Y., May 2016 22

2016: Here We Are on the Brink 23

In memory of Charles F. Lauter (1890—1980)
Private, Corporal, Sargent and Second Lt.,
Battery B of the 306th Field Artillery
77th Division, U.S. Army, American Expeditionary Force,
1917-1919

Military Record:
Baccarat Sector, July 20-August 4, 1918
The Champagne-Marne Defensive
Vesle Sector, August 4-August 18, 1918
Oise-Aisne, August 18-September 1, 1918
Meuse-Argonne Offensive, September 26-November 11, 1918
Saumur Artillery School, Saumur, France,
September 1-November 23, 1918

Preface

The story at the heart of these poems, about the effects of war on the men who didn't speak about it, is one that can never be fully known, but in this case, it has at least been possible to reconstruct most of what happened to one man in World War I from September 1917—May 1919. A group of seven soldiers in his unit, stuck in France for five months after the Armistice with no mission, pooled their memories, records and photos to write *The Story of Battery B, 306th F.A.—77th Division*. One of their officers, Lt. Roswell A. De La Mater, had the book printed in New York after they returned home. In it, they described in detail what they had actually experienced. Their history differs from both popular and official histories of WWI in many ways, probably because those versions tend not to focus on Artillery men who worked in teams to clear the way for Infantry. These men had little opportunity for heroism, but they were nonetheless essential to the Allied victory. This book seeks to reconstruct the story of one of these men.

Legacy
    For Charles Lauterwasser*

When you cut the *wasser* from the family name
insisting that you were born American,
scratched the *wasser* off family medals
and tombstones, burned your papers of origin,

enlisted in the U.S. Army for the war
to end all wars against your *Vaterland*,
did you think your children
would never want to know

if their forbears had lautered beer
or purified water, if they were louder
because they lived beside a waterfall
or clearer because they lived by a spring?

Did you think your father's homeland
could never be redeemed
and the new world would never
make the same mistakes?

You never said.
We didn't ask

*The word "lauter" in German can mean louder, more clear or more pure. The British refer to one process in making beer as lautering. "Wasser" means water.

The Thin Red Book
> *The Story of Battery B: 306th Field Artillery—77th Division, September 21, 1917-May 10, 1919. N.Y.: Premier Printing Co., 1919*

Nineteen months gone from your life.
We knew you'd been to war in France.
You talked about your stint at Saumur,
becoming an officer on horseback.
About the chateau where you stayed
when you were briefly lost. Mentioned
names of a few buddies and Captain Fine.

Now, we read the stories you didn't tell
in a thin red book with glossy pages,
black and white photos and drawings,
a single printing for members only.
Written by seven soldiers waiting
together, impatiently, to go home
long after the Armistice was signed.

About a field artillery unit
that trained on Long Island
one fall and winter.

About a spring voyage on the Leviathan,
entry at Brest and a march to a decrepit
Napoleonic camp. Then train-rides south
to a working camp with guns and masks
and diagonally across France to the front.

We found maps to follow your routes
to Lorraine, then back toward Paris
and on to the Argonne. A shell landed
between two horses pulling a gun
(but your casualty page is missing).
The pattern repeated seven times
from July to November. Then the wait
for a ship to go home. *And finally,*
the parade with all your cousins watching.

How could you keep the book for 60 years,
bringing it with you when you came
to live in our home, reading it so often
the spine is worn, but never tell us
what happened to you
in this war that changed
our century, your life, ours?

German American

Born in New Jersey, you grew up
among the *Krauts* in Carlstadt
and moved across the Hudson
to start a business, own a boat,
live a good life partying
on Long Island Sound,
when German troops in Belgium
struck a nerve. Suddenly
the field of enemies narrowed
and *they* were *you*.

You laid down the law: *keine
Zeitungen*, no German newspapers,
no more conversations *auf Deutsch*.
You organized the family
to change its name,
make it sound Scottish.

Then the *Lusitania* went down,
outrage grew to Declaration
and you were in the Army
to save the family honor
—cousins all girls,
your brother sick
from breathing foul air
working for U.S. Customs
in Manhattan's Battery.

All American to the core.

Camp Upton, 1917

You joined the new National Army,
headed out to Long Island
to be trained by green officers
who began their posts with *nothing*,

no artillery, horses, wagons
not even tents or latrines.

Together you built barracks,
modeled the big guns with logs,
imaged horses with two-by-fours,
made caissons from feed boxes,
and when all this was done,
took long hikes to build endurance.

For seven months, you drilled
for unity, learned signaling with flags,
shot rifles at targets, did endless
calisthenics, without ever loading
a Howitzer, feeding or hitching
a horse, wearing a gas mask.

It must have driven you crazy.

You were a man who kept his tools
in order, on hand, ready for use
in a thriving electrical business
on Washington Square, where
O. Henry exchanged his books
for your services.

You probably strung lights for the new barracks
in your spare time, made the best of a bad scene.

The USS Leviathan

Named for a Biblical sea monster,
the ship had a mess for 10,000
and so many decks the officers
printed directions on stairwells
to prevent men from getting lost.
You slept on four-tiered stretchers.

By day you learned how to go
overboard if a sub attacked
—not enough life-boats for all,
so Battery B was assigned to rafts.
Swimming was not among
the family *Turnverein* medals.

Everyone stood duty—kitchen,
garbage, guard—while destroyers
stood by the ship itself on the ten-day
voyage to the coast of France,
where you piled into British *lighters*
for a rocky ride to shore.

Despite your poor preparation
you were greeted with cries
of V*ive l'Amerique,* hounded
by children with requests
for chocolate and *cigarettes*
for *ze papa.*

Trials Galore, April—July, 1918

Right off the boat, a six-mile hike
from Brest to Napoleon's bedless barracks
where Americans had already made
a baseball diamond. Since you had broken
every finger playing ball by then
you were probably first on that field.

Then you went south in a box car
to Camp de Souge near Bordeaux
to drill ten hours a day for just
two months with real Howitzers
and horses, firefights, gas and masks.
The months of make-believe were over.

But not until the first Defensive
on the eastern front did you actually dig
emplacements for guns, build platforms
and ditches, cover them with foliage.
Supplies came at night so you learned
to divide flour, sugar and coffee in the dark.

In fifteen days at Baccarat, with ten months
of bumbling behind you, you forged a chain
of gunners, drivers, phone and radio teams,
blacksmiths, mechanics, cooks, buglers,
orderlies, and of course, always, horses.
You were finally prepared.

Forty Men or Eight Horses

What did you think when you saw the train
that would take you to Bordeaux and then
across the heart of France to Alsace-Lorraine?

Box cars marked *Les Hommes: Quarante,*
ou *Les Cheveaux: Huit.* Box cars were
for hobos and you had come to fight a war.

You would soon stand like horses, or take turns
kneeling, crouching, sitting, almost never lying down.
A slow journey with hours between stops

rarely seeing light because the cars
were camouflage. *No one* was supposed
to see that foreign troops were under way.

German airmen flying low could not tell
what was in those windowless cars
and might not waste their fire on cargo.

Even without knowing the way such cars
would be used in the next war, weren't you
just a bit afraid to step aboard?

The Baccarat Decanter

By mid-July Battery B was in Baccarat,
with French and German heritage
where trust was worn thin by spies.

In one of your stories, you told how,
separated by accident, you spent
an anxious night with the family

that founded Baccarat glass, how they
gave you a chit for their New York store
where you later claimed a wine decanter.

Did you choose it or did the family
choose it for you to remind you
of what France meant to them?

The fleur-de-lis so prominent
in its bowl, the neck so thin, the handle
graceful as a bride, the stopper luminous.

An odd choice for a German-American bachelor
who never drank wine except at communion,
no bride in sight. But maybe after the Armistice

while you waited in desperate French towns
you shared a glass or two with men in a café?
There must have been wine left in the cellars

and having just vanquished *Jerry**
you probably would not have admitted
your preference for beer.

*The Allies had several derogatory names for German soldiers,
among them, *Boche, Fritz, Huns, Jerry and Kraut.*

Proving Your Worth

By mid-August, you had moved west
to put your practice to the test
half-way between Soissons and Reims
near the famous Chateau-Thierry
where the French had taken heavy fire.

German troops were in retreat,
their bombers bent on stopping
your offensives. The stench
from shallow graves was sickening,
the ground littered with human debris.

Your kitchen was hit three times.
You watched two American planes
come down and buried the pilots.
Two men in Battery B were killed.
You marked their graves with crosses.

Chasing the *Huns* from the Vesle River
to the Aisne, your battalion set records
for speed from receipt of an order
to release of ammunition, rarely knowing
what the new coordinates marked.

Suddenly, you were tapped
for promotion. Sent for part
of the next three months
to the Loire Valley
to *study* war.

After the Vesle

The records put you in two places at once,
still part of the famous Argonne Offensive
but also enrolled in courses at Saumur,
the French Artillery Officers Training School.

The *Fritz* had held the Argonne Forest between the valleys
of Aire and Aisne for three long years, laced
with barbed wire and decorated with machine-gun nests
behind the infamous Hindenberg Line.*

Your book says that guns regrouped *like things of life,
crouching like huge beasts to spring upon their prey,*
until Artillery had to defer to Infantry,
simply stand by to communicate
with watching aeroplanes and balloons, until the *Boche
ran like an overpowering wave, dashing for home.*

I hope you felt no guilt or shame in leaving.
If your officers had known when this war would end
they would never have sent you out of battle.

---

*By 1918, the Germans had created four "lines" of barbed wire, mines, and other means of protecting themselves as they advanced across France. The Hindenberg Line was their first line of defense as they advanced and the last as they retreated.

The Eight-Day March, September 1918
> *It was the fastest trip by artillery for that distance*
> *ever made in any war by any artillery.*
> *From the thin red book*

We'll never know if you were there
when, night after night they marched
on foot for a drive that they hoped
would get them home by Christmas,
marched across land that had seen
four years of battle, torn by thousands
of hooves, cut by wheels, packed
by heavy boots then drenched in rain.

Spattered with mud, men slept by day
in forests or branch-covered ditches,
under the watchful eye of German planes,
and marched more-than-one-hundred
miles by night to the Argonne Forest.

Were you there at the River Marne
when they stole a silent daytime swim
or when they formed bucket-brigades
to water the horses, or set up tents
and threw down an overcoat
on the clay-like mud to sleep?

Were you there when horses dropped
along the road, a man miss-stepped
under a caisson wheel and the kitchen
did not arrive for meals? Or the night
when, on a narrow forest trail,
men wondered if their tired horses
would slip and fall into the deep ravine?

Found Poetry

On the first day of the Argonne offensive,
Battery B had one gun for every eight meters
along the German line to cut sixteen avenues
through thick webs of barbed wire.
Your buddies remembered in soldier's tongue:

> *One set of guns was to lay a rolling barrage*
> *500 meters ahead, while another set*
> *placed a protective barrage 500 meters*
> *in front of that one. For twenty-five minutes,*
> *both barrages were to be advanced*
> *by one-hundred-meter jumps every five minutes.*

But the results required poetry:

> *[That night] the sky was splashed*
> *with bloody red as an avalanche of steel*
> *tore and bit its way through space*
> *to the German line ahead. Great hungry*
> *tongues of fire licked the blackness of the night.*

Some days the men could not see where
to shoot and some nights they had to pull
four-ton guns through mud and shell-holes
at six hours per half-mile until they reached
the *great German line of defense* with its
trenches and concrete pill-boxes.

Apparently the Boche expected to stay forever.
The bunkers that had not been smashed
were fitted with hardwood floors, fireplaces,
fancy wallpaper and electric lights.

For the rest of October into November,
our big guns helped the doughboys along.

One of the few stories

you told was about the Training School at Saumur where you were sent to advance in skills and rank. We have your report card for *Topography, Telephone, Radio & Telegraph, Dispersion and Ballistics, Artillery Ammunition, Preparation and Execution of Fire,* along with *Equitation and Hippology.*

There were thousands of horses in this war, but you were a city boy, a tailor's son, so riding and tending horses was not in your genes. All grades except the last were high—even in *Deportment and Conduct* (maybe you didn't wise-crack in French).

One day, you said, the riding instructor assigned you a horse that bolted, taking you over fences, brooks and stone walls at a gallop, and when you returned from this test, he said *Ah, Sar-geant, you give her be-au-ti-ful ride,* then added in a conspiratorial tone, *You know, she used to be mine.*

When you asked him *why
did you give her up,* he sighed
Ahhh, but she stumbles.

Unintended Consequences

The Argonne was the Allied Army's final test in France
but no one knew this when the men of Battery B
boarded box cars to ride across France.
No one knew whether the giant Howitzers

would make it through the forest
under horse-power, protect the Infantry,
keep the enemy on the run,
disabled, knotted in pain and fear.

No one knew how many days and nights they would fire
to penetrate the enemy's *faux* homes, furnished with bathtubs,
impractical even for removing lice, those miserable parasites,
hideous pests both sides would hate almost as much as bullets.

New blood, moral outrage and innocence were on our side
underneath the helmets, inside the gas masks
at Vesle, Aisne and in the once-pristine Argonne Forest
where the enemy was finally imprisoned, Xed out,

or sent back across the border to the *Vaterland*.
No one knew how the ones who got away would yearn
for dominance, smart from defeat, ears full of zooming planes
and the rush that came from winning for so long.

After the Armistice

you waited in makeshift barracks,
with dirt floors, leaky roofs and wet wood
for fuel. Bathed under a crude shower
in a small shed on the river banks of damaged
towns mostly too small to show up in our atlas.
Waited for a ship and release from quarantine.

Some of your men replayed war problems
or provided holiday cheer for villagers,
but seven of them wrote a book
from memory, diaries, records
of rounds fired, orders received,
kilometers walked, horses lost.

They didn't present you as heroes,
spoke with admiration of Infantry men,
especially the *Lost Battalion*
who fought hand-to-hand, relentlessly,
refusing to retreat when they began to fall.
But we couldn't have won without Artillery.

Major General Robert Alexander
would honor you at home in May by saying:

> *These men . . . have been welded*
> *into as powerful a unit of war*
> *as has been marshalled*
> *on [any] field of battle.*

You were there.
It was your story to tell.

Homecoming
From The Story of Battery B

After your year in France, you boarded the *USS Agamemnon*,
formerly Kaiser Wilhelm II, where aside from cleaning details
you had a gala time, singing, boxing, listening to music.
On April 28th, you were up at 4 a. m. looking for land—
Coney Island,
   South Brooklyn,
      The Old Girl Herself,
         Governors Island,
            the New York skyline like castles in the air.

Ferries, police craft, boats packed with families and friends
crowded the harbor singing *Home Sweet Home, Smiles,*
even *Dixie.* You were showered with newspapers, oranges,
chocolate. The Red Cross in Hoboken prepared a hot meal.
Then five days of torture in tents at Fort Mills where you were
de-loused for the last time before boarding a train to the city
for the big parade on May 6th to honor 22,000 men of the 77th—
the Statue of Liberty Division.

From you, we know only that your sister Henrietta and favorite
cousins Helen, Frieda and Len were in the sidelines. Your shop
on Washington Square was sold, your brother moved upstate
to a farm for his health. Whatever you may have felt that day,
despite a promotion and kudos from Cap'n Fine,
you did not stay in the Army.

Task done
       identity secured
              nationality won.

The Photo Enigma

Two loose photos of the same fourteen men survive,
one with names, but neither labeled by place or date.

The photo with no names is posed
ironically before a tank you never rode
the men dressed up in long winter coats
gloves, wide-brim hats with high crowns.
Some hold certificates, looking pleased,
but you are the only one who grins.
Still a bit of a daredevil, *n'est ce pas?*
Probably your graduation from Saumur,
23 November 1918.

In the picture with carefully printed names
and American cities on the back,
a *carte postale* you never sent,
you are all seated outside on the stairs
of a rundown public building in jackets
and scuffed boots, legs every which way.
Despite some half-smiles
you all look worn to the bone.

Larry, Philip, Henry, Hugh, Paul;
three men named Charles,
three Franks, two Ernests,
and one Jolley, whose other name
you did not recall. Classmates.
At last, I see a stray word in tiny print:
home.

The Spoils of War

Your son, born twenty years later,
remembers a German helmet, *Ein Pickelhaube,*
made of hardened leather with a spike
at the crown and metal trim to form an eagle,
gear that should have been abandoned
by 1914 because it did not protect the head.

You never sold it, though it was worth big money,
so why did you bring it back? You must have found it
in one of the ruined bunkers from which you chased
German men who could have been your relatives.
Put it in your pack and carried it on foot, how far?
An officer's helmet. Your counterpart.

The sidearm you brought back, Smith and Wesson
or Colt, stayed on a shelf and disappeared
when your house was sold in the Sixties.
Having learned to shoot both rifles and Howitzers,
you had no appetite for guns. If your pals in the Legion
continued their target practice, they did so without you.
The brother-in-law who lived down the street hunted alone.

And the only word of possible German origin
we ever heard you say was *snickelfritz,*
a term of endearment for children.

Why Didn't You Speak?

Maybe you wanted to protect us
from the poisons of war.

Maybe you were indignant with the Army
and your country for their failure
to provide essential support
for the men they sent to war.

But I fear there was another *raison d'etre:*
the loss of the person you were before the war
the *German-*American, talented athlete, carefree
bachelor, skilled electrician, leader of men

as if your former life
were tarnished
to the point of never
being shineable again

as if you'd lived
one life to age 28
and it was over in 1919
when a new one began

in which you were
a farmer, factory worker,
husband, father, air-raid warden,
churchman, citizen, grandfather

as if the legs had been cut out
from under you (and ironically
you were lame at sixty, cartilage
in your hips and knees all gone).

I grieve for what you lost.
Thank heavens it was not
your whole life.

The Amnesia of War

You never spoke about the war
although it changed your life.
We didn't ask about the war
although it made ours possible.

It would have been unseemly.
You were a half-century older
settled in your bones
rickety as they were

with enough sorrows
—the early deaths
of your brother, George
and the love of your life, Ione.

If we had reproved you
I can imagine your shrug,
accompanied by
an unreadable smile.

But it didn't occur to us
to ask the simplest question
about the stories you told:
What happened then?

And having missed our chance
will we forever
need to search
this troubled history?

Aftermath: Greene, N.Y., May, 2016

When did you become a modest man?

Was it when you proved
what you had set out to prove
and felt secure?

You were American.
Was there nothing left
to say compared with that?

Your name is on the monument
in this small, upstate town where you
settled in May, 1919, on a farm

hating every minute
of *playing nursemaid to a cow,*
but you built a life for us.

There we were, four generations
of the family you tended,
speaking of you.

2016: Here We Are on the Brink

Not quite one hundred years
after the Great War did not
end all wars

Not quite one hundred years
after the Treaty of Versailles
drew impossible borders

Not quite one hundred years
after Hitler's brown shirts
muscled into power

Not quite one hundred years
after the fantasy of Aryan
purity took hold

Not quite one hundred years
after so-called undesirables
were shunted into camps

Here we are on the brink.

Since her retirement from the University of Wisconsin Oshkosh as Chair of the English Department, **Estella** has reveled in writing poetry, publishing three chapbooks with Finishing Line Press (one of them in the New Women's Voices series). Her poems have won awards from the Wisconsin Fellowship of Poets (WFOP), the Wisconsin Writers Association, *Fox Cry* and the *Peninsula Pulse*. She tied for first prize in the 2009 Barbara Mandigo Kelly Peace Poetry contest, and her work has been published in several literary journals, including *Free Verse, Verse Wisconsin, Wisconsin People and Ideas, Bramble* and *Midwest Review*. Two poems were nominated for the Pushcart award. Poems have also appeared in several anthologies, including *The Nature of Door, Sweeping Beauty,* and *Echolocations.*

Estella served as Poet Laureate of Door County in 2013-2015, during which time she founded the Door County Poets Collective to publish an anthology, *Soundings: Door County in Poetry* (Caravaggio Press, 2015). Most recently, she co-edited the 2017 Poets Calendar for WFOP on the theme of water. She has begun to offer workshops on travel poetry and political poetry for Write On Door County, and she continues to explore relationships between poetry and the arts. In this period of political crisis, she is grateful to be part of a vital community of poets and to live on 31 acres of woodland near Lake Michigan with her husband, Charles Lauter.

www.ingramcontent.com/pod-product-compliance
Lightning Source LLC
LaVergne TN
LVHW041518070426
835507LV00012B/1664